Number 12
on Periodic
Table

S0-BRD-458

WITHDRAWN
No longer the property of the
Boston Public Library.
Sale of this material benefits the Library

# SPARKS OF LIFE

Chemical Elements that Make Life Possible

# MAGNESIUM

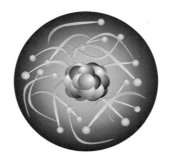

by

Jean F. Blashfield

RAINTREE
STECK-VAUGHN
PUBLISHERS

A Harcourt Company

Austin   New York
www.raintreesteckvaughn.com

Special thanks to our technical consultant,
Philip T. Johns, Ph.D.
University of Wisconsin—Whitewater, Wisconsin

**Copyright ©2002, Raintree Steck-Vaughn Publishers**
All rights reserved. No part of the material protected by this copyright may be reproduced or utilized in any form or by any means, electronic or mechanical, including photocopying, recording, or by any information storage and retrieval system, without permission in writing from the copyright owner. Requests for permission to make copies of any part of the work should be mailed to: Copyright Permission, Raintree Steck-Vaughn Publishers, P. O. Box 26015, Austin, TX 78755.

**Development: Books Two, Inc., Delavan, Wisconsin**
> Graphics: Krueger Graphics, Janesville, Wisconsin
> Interior Design: Peg Esposito
> Photo Research: Margie Benson
> Indexing: Winston E. Black

**Raintree Steck-Vaughn Publisher's Staff:**
> Publishing Director: Walter Kossmann    Project Editor
> Design Manager: Richard A. Johnson

UC BR
J
QD181
.M4B53
2002

**Library of Congress Cataloging-in-Publication Data:**
Blashfield, Jean F.

Magnesium / by Jean F. Blashfield.
   p. cm. — (Sparks of life)
Includes bibliographical references and index.
ISBN 0-7398-4360-5
   1. Magnesium--Juvenile literature. 2. Magnesium--Physiological aspects--Juvenile literature. [1. Magnesium.] I. Title.

QD181.M4. B53 2001
546'.392--dc21                                                    2001019555

Printed and bound in the United States
1 2 3 4 5 6 7 8 9 LB 05 04 03 02 01

PHOTO CREDITS: Archive Photos 9; B.I.F.C. cover; ©Jonathan Blair/CORBIS 19; ©Jean B. Black  24; ©Martin Bond/Science Photo Library 56; ©Steve Callahan/Visuals Unlimited 45; Culligan International Company 23; ©Dr. E. R. Derringer 34; ©Phil Degginger 53, cover (2); Dow Chemical 32, 47, 50; ©Michael Eichelberger/Visuals Unlimited 28; Ford Motor Co. 51; ©Simon Fraser/Royal Victoria Infirmary, Newcastle/Science Photo Library 41; ©Irving Geis/Peter Arnold, Inc. 32; ©George Gerster/PhotoResearchers 26; ©Jeff Greenberg/Visuals Unlimited 39; Richard P. Jacobs/JLM Visuals 15, 18; ©Breck P. Kent/JLM Visuals 17; ©Leonard Lessin/Peter Arnold, Inc.  11; Magnesium Corp. 48; ©David Newman/Visuals Unlimited 30; NASA 14; Norsk Hydro 54; OAR/National Undersea Research Program 52; ©David M. Phillips/Visuals Unlimited  cover; ©Harry J. Przekop, Stock Shop/Medichrome cover; ©SIV/Visuals Unlimited 40; ©Larry Stepanowicz/Visuals Unlimited 12; ©Rich Treptow 1987/Visuals Unlimited 49; USDA Agricultural Research Service 29, 31, 43; ©William J. Weber/Visuals Unlimited 44; Photo courtesy of Wickman Spacecraft & Propulsion Company 57; ©Georgette Douwma/FPG 52

# CONTENTS

Mg

# Periodic Table of the Elements

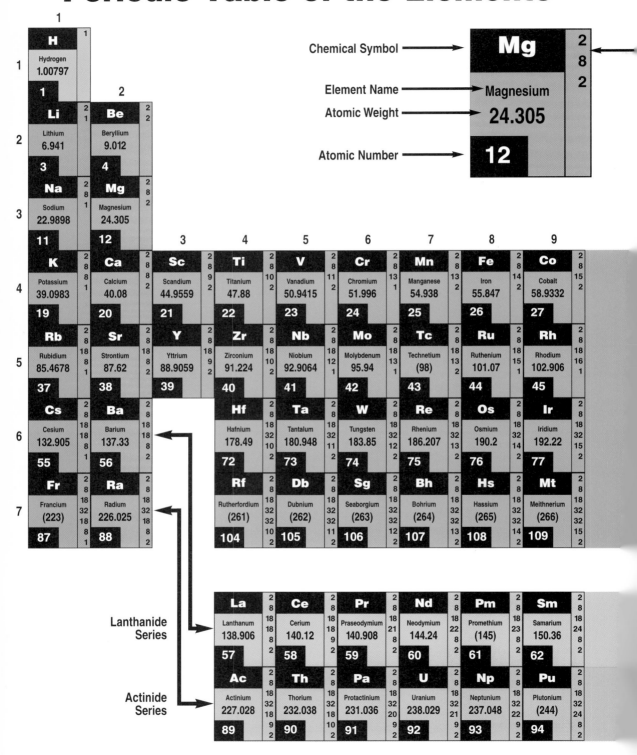

Number of electrons in each shell, beginning with the K shell, top.

See next page for explanations.

| Group | 13 | 14 | 15 | 16 | 17 | 18 |
|---|---|---|---|---|---|---|
| | | | | | | **He** Helium 4.0026 — 2 |
| | **B** Boron 10.81 — 2,3 — 5 | **C** Carbon 12.011 — 2,4 — 6 | **N** Nitrogen 14.0067 — 2,5 — 7 | **O** Oxygen 15.9994 — 2,6 — 8 | **F** Fluorine 18.9984 — 2,7 — 9 | **Ne** Neon 20.179 — 2,8 — 10 |
| | **Al** Aluminum 26.9815 — 2,8,3 — 13 | **Si** Silicon 28.0855 — 2,8,4 — 14 | **P** Phosphorus 30.9738 — 2,8,5 — 15 | **S** Sulfur 32.06 — 2,8,6 — 16 | **Cl** Chlorine 35.453 — 2,8,7 — 17 | **Ar** Argon 39.948 — 2,8,8 — 18 |

| 10 | 11 | 12 | 13 | 14 | 15 | 16 | 17 | 18 |
|---|---|---|---|---|---|---|---|---|
| **Ni** Nickel 58.69 — 2,8,16,2 — 28 | **Cu** Copper 63.546 — 2,8,18,1 — 29 | **Zn** Zinc 65.39 — 2,8,18,2 — 30 | **Ga** Gallium 69.72 — 2,8,18,3 — 31 | **Ge** Germanium 72.59 — 2,8,18,4 — 32 | **As** Arsenic 74.9216 — 2,8,18,5 — 33 | **Se** Selenium 78.96 — 2,8,18,6 — 34 | **Br** Bromine 79.904 — 2,8,18,7 — 35 | **Kr** Krypton 83.80 — 2,8,18,8 — 36 |
| **Pd** Palladium 106.42 — 2,8,18,18 — 46 | **Ag** Silver 107.868 — 2,8,18,18,1 — 47 | **Cd** Cadmium 112.41 — 2,8,18,18,2 — 48 | **In** Indium 114.82 — 2,8,18,18,3 — 49 | **Sn** Tin 118.71 — 2,8,18,18,4 — 50 | **Sb** Antimony 121.75 — 2,8,18,18,5 — 51 | **Te** Tellurium 127.6 — 2,8,18,18,6 — 52 | **I** Iodine 126.905 — 2,8,18,18,7 — 53 | **Xe** Xenon 131.29 — 2,8,18,18,8 — 54 |
| **Pt** Platinum 195.08 — 2,8,18,32,17,1 — 78 | **Au** Gold 196.967 — 2,8,18,32,18,1 — 79 | **Hg** Mercury 200.59 — 2,8,18,32,18,2 — 80 | **Tl** Thallium 204.383 — 2,8,18,32,18,3 — 81 | **Pb** Lead 207.2 — 2,8,18,32,18,4 — 82 | **Bi** Bismuth 208.98 — 2,8,18,32,18,5 — 83 | **Po** Polonium (209) — 2,8,18,32,18,6 — 84 | **At** Astatine (210) — 2,8,18,32,18,7 — 85 | **Rn** Radon (222) — 2,8,18,32,18,8 — 86 |
| **(Uun)** (Ununnilium) (269) — 2,8,18,32,32,17,1 — 110 | **(Unu)** (Unununium) (272) — 2,8,18,32,32,18,1 — 111 | **(Uub)** (Ununbium) (277) — 2,8,18,32,32,18,2 — 112 | | | | | | |

**COLOR KEYS**

Alkali Metals | Transition Metals | Nonmetals | Metalloids | Lanthanide Series

Alkaline Earth Metals | Other Metals | Noble Gases | Actinide Series

| | | | | | | | | |
|---|---|---|---|---|---|---|---|---|
| **Eu** Europium 151.96 — 2,8,18,25,8,2 — 63 | **Gd** Gadolinium 157.25 — 2,8,18,25,9,2 — 64 | **Tb** Terbium 158.925 — 2,8,18,27,8,2 — 65 | **Dy** Dysprosium 162.50 — 2,8,18,28,8,2 — 66 | **Ho** Holmium 164.93 — 2,8,18,29,8,2 — 67 | **Er** Erbium 167.26 — 2,8,18,30,8,2 — 68 | **Tm** Thulium 168.934 — 2,8,18,31,8,2 — 69 | **Yb** Ytterbium 173.04 — 2,8,18,32,8,2 — 70 | **Lu** Lutetium 174.967 — 2,8,18,32,9,2 — 71 |
| **Am** Americium (243) — 2,8,18,32,25,8,2 — 95 | **Cm** Curium (247) — 2,8,18,32,25,9,2 — 96 | **Bk** Berkelium (247) — 2,8,18,32,26,9,2 — 97 | **Cf** Californium (251) — 2,8,18,32,28,8,2 — 98 | **Es** Einsteinium (254) — 2,8,18,32,29,8,2 — 99 | **Fm** Fermium (257) — 2,8,18,32,30,8,2 — 100 | **Md** Mendelevium (258) — 2,8,18,32,31,8,2 — 101 | **No** Nobelium (259) — 2,8,18,32,32,8,2 — 102 | **Lr** Lawrencium (260) — 2,8,18,32,32,9,2 — 103 |

# A Guide to the Periodic Table

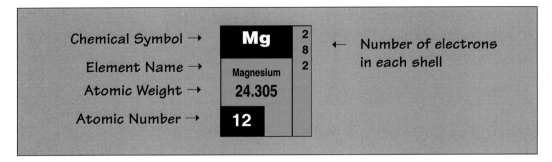

**Symbol =** an abbreviation of an element name, agreed on by members of the International Union of Pure and Applied Chemistry. The idea to use symbols was started by a Swedish chemist, Jöns Jakob Berzelius, about 1814. Note that the elements with numbers 110, 111, and 112, which were "discovered" in 1996, have not yet been given official names.

**Atomic number =** the number of protons (particles with a positive electrical charge) in the nucleus of an atom of an element; also equal to the number of electrons (particles with a negative electrical charge) found in the shells, or rings, of an atom that does not have an electrical charge.

**Atomic weight =** the weight of an element compared to carbon. When the Periodic Table was first developed, hydrogen was used as the standard. It was given an atomic weight of 1, but that created some difficulties, and in 1962, the standard was changed to carbon-12, which is the most common form of the element carbon, with an atomic weight of 12.

The Periodic Table on pages 4 and 5 shows the atomic weight of carbon as 12.011 because an atomic weight is an average of the weights, or masses, of all the different naturally occurring forms of an atom. Each form, called an isotope, has a different number of neutrons (uncharged particles) in the nucleus. Most elements have several isotopes, but chemists assume that any two samples of an element are made up of the same mixture of isotopes and thus have the same mass, or weight.

**Electron shells =** regions surrounding the nucleus of an atom in which the electrons move. Historically, electron shells have been described as orbits similar to a planet's orbit. But actually they are whole areas of a specific energy level, in which certain electrons vibrate and move around. The shell closest to the nucleus, the K shell, can contain only 2 electrons. The K shell has the lowest energy level, and it is very hard to break its electrons away. The second shell, L, can contain only 8 electrons. Others may contain up to 32 electrons. The outer shell, in which chemical reactions occur, is called the valence shell.

**Periods =** horizontal rows of elements in the Periodic Table. A period contains all the elements with the same number of orbital shells of electrons. Note that the actinide and lanthanide (or rare earth) elements shown in rows below the main table really belong within the table, but it is not regarded as practical to print such a wide table as would be required.

**Groups =** vertical columns of elements in the Periodic Table; also called families. A group contains all elements that naturally have the same number of electrons in the outermost shell or orbital of the atom. Elements in a group tend to behave in similar ways.

Group 1 = alkali metals: very reactive and so never found in nature in their pure form. Bright, soft metals, they have one valence electron and, like all metals, conduct both electricity and heat.

Group 2 = alkaline earth metals: also very reactive and thus don't occur pure in nature. Harder and denser than alkali metals, they have two valence electrons that easily combine with other chemicals.

Groups 3–12 = transition metals: the great mass of metals, with a variable number of electrons; can exist in pure form.

Groups 13–17 = transition metals, metalloids, and nonmetals. Metalloids possess some characteristics of metals and some of nonmetals. Unlike metals and metalloids, nonmetals do not conduct electricity.

Group 18 = noble, or rare, gases: in general, these nonmetallic gaseous elements do not react with other elements because their valence shells are full.

# TAKING THE WATERS

In 1618 in the town of Epsom, England, a farmer's cows refused to drink from a spring that had bubbled up in one of his fields. When the farmer tasted the water, he, too, found that it tasted bad. However, the water helped to heal scratches and a rash on his skin. Also, when he drank a lot of the spring water, it worked as a laxative—a substance that speeds the emptying of the bowels.

The word spread about these marvelous waters, and a health resort, or spa, was built at Epsom where people could visit and "take the waters." Spas were popular in Europe, but this was the first one that had been located in England.

Over the next two centuries, several researchers came to Epsom to investigate the healthful waters. In 1695, Nehemiah Grew, a physician, identified the laxative substance in the water at Epsom. He called the mineral he separated out Epsom salts, but he did not yet know exactly what it was.

Another mineral in the waters at Epsom was separated out in 1755 by Scottish physician and chemist Joseph Black. Black called it magnesia. But just what magnesia and Epsom salts were made of remained a puzzle.

## Davy's Incredible Element-Discovering Machine

Fifty years later, English chemist Humphry Davy set about solving the mystery. It was just one in a series of scientific mysteries he was investigating by conducting electricity through different fluid substances. Called electrolysis, this process caused some compounds to decompose, or break up, into the elements contained in them.

**Sir Humphry Davy**

At the heart of Davy's device was an electric battery, which was being developed by Italian physicist Alessandro Volta. Soon after the development of the "voltaic cell" was announced, it was used by English chemist William Nicholson to break water into its two components, oxygen (O, element #8) and hydrogen (H, #1).

Excited at learning of this application of electricity, Davy set about analyzing many different substances, using electrolysis to break them apart. Soon he had identified several new chemical elements, including potassium (K, for *kalium,* element #19), sodium (Na, for *natrium,* #11), barium (Ba, #56), strontium (Sr, #38), and calcium (Ca, #20).

To use his device, Davy attached the battery between two bars, called electrodes, of different

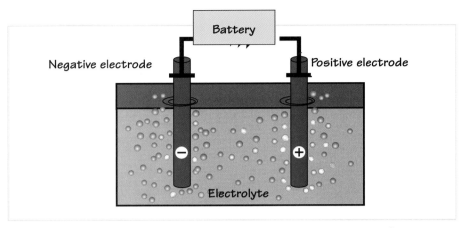

**Humphry Davy isolated magnesium by using a mixture of magnesia and mercuric oxide as the electrolyte.**

metals, which were immersed in the fluid being tested—the electrolyte. An electrolyte contains ions, which are atoms or other particles that are missing electrons or have extra electrons. Negative ions are negative because they have more electrons than there are positive protons in the nucleus. Positive ions have fewer electrons than protons.

When Davy turned the battery on, electricity flowed into the electrolyte. Electricity consists of a flow of electrons. The positive ions—cations—moved to the cathode, the negative electrode. The negatively charged ions—anions—flowed to the positive electrode, or anode.

In 1808, Davy was still testing substances that puzzled him. In one test, he used a mixture of magnesia and mercuric oxide as the electrolyte. (Mercury is Hg, for *hydrargyrum*—meaning "liquid silver," element #80.) At first, the mercury and the magnesia just formed another mixture, called an amalgam, but when Davy heated the amalgam, the mercury turned into a vapor and bubbled out, leaving a silvery metal behind.

Davy quickly found that the common ingredient in both Epsom salts and magnesia was the silvery metal, an element he called magnesium. He later identified Epsom salts as magnesium sulfate, $MgSO_4$ (sulfur is S, element #16), and magnesia, or magnesium oxide, MgO.

Today, Epsom's spa no longer exists. The town is now better known for its world-famous racetrack, Epsom Downs, but Epsom salts remain in medicine cabinets all over the world.

Epsom salts dissolved in water soothe aching and swollen feet.

## Element Number 12

Magnesium has an atomic number of 12. That means it has 12 protons, or positively charged particles, in the nucleus. They are balanced by 12 electrons, negative particles that move in shells, or orbits, around the nucleus. Also in the nucleus are a number of electrically neutral particles called neutrons. The number of neutrons in natural magnesium can vary from 12 to 14.

Magnesium is located in the second column of the Periodic Table of the Elements. Elements in Group 2 (also called Group IIA) have two electrons in their outer, or valence, orbits. Other elements in Group 2 include beryllium (Be, element #4), calcium, strontium, barium, and radium (Ra, #88).

Group 2 elements are called alkaline-earth metals, a name left over from long ago. Alchemists were researchers in the Middle Ages who believed that substances could be changed by a combination of science, magic, and religion. Alchemists called certain rocks alkaline "earths," in the belief that they were fundamental substances of Earth. Scientists later found that these rocks were not elements but metal oxides, which are substances combining a metallic element and oxygen. However, the metals contained in these oxides are still called alkaline-earth metals.

Atoms of the alkaline-earth metals easily give up the two electrons in their valence shells in order to become stable. They become positive ions, written $Mg^{2+}$. Magnesium is thus regarded as a reactive metal. It reacts most easily with oxygen, which has six electrons in its outer orbit. Because an atom can become stable with eight valence electrons, oxygen readily takes on those two outer electrons from magnesium, which willingly gives them up. The result is an electrically neutral substance called magnesium oxide.

## The Fiery Metal

**Metallic magnesium burns with a brilliant white light in air.**

The ease with which magnesium reacts with oxygen means that it flames easily. The pure metal can be used only in places where the temperature does not get very hot. It ignites at 650°C (1,202°F).

Never look directly at magnesium when you know it's about to be ignited. It burns with a brilliant flare that can permanently damage the retina of your eyes.

The flaring, bright-white light of burning powdered magnesium was once used to provide light for indoor photography. The powder burned vigorously, often burning the photographer. Other solutions were found for photography, but the powder is still added to fireworks to increase the brightness of the colors against the night sky.

Firebombs made of magnesium were once dropped on cities to set fire to them and to provide light for bombers to find their targets. Cities in Europe and Japan, such as Dresden and Tokyo, were firebombed in World War II (1939–1945). They suffered terrible damage.

Once a magnesium fire starts, it cannot be put out with water because its atoms will react with the oxygen and hydrogen in the water, releasing hydrogen gas and making the fire worse. Instead, a magnesium fire must be smothered with sand or dirt.

## Important Compounds

Magnesia, or magnesium oxide, MgO, is the second most abundant compound in Earth's crust. Only sand—silicon dioxide, $SiO_2$—is more plentiful. (Silicon is Si, element #14.) It's estimated that 33 percent of the rocks on Earth include magnesium oxide in their makeup.

In the ocean, 0.13 percent of the water is magnesium, in the form of magnesium chloride, $MgCl_2$. (Chlorine is Cl, element #17.) Seawater is the source of most magnesium used today.

## Isotopes

All atoms of an element must have the same number of protons in the nucleus to actually be that element. However, different atoms can have different numbers of neutrons—particles with no charge—in the nucleus and still be the same element. These atoms with different numbers of neutrons are called isotopes of the element. All isotopes of one element belong in the same place in the Periodic Table of the Elements. *Isotope* means "same place."

More than three-quarters of naturally occurring magnesium has 12 neutrons, written Mg-24 (12 neutrons plus 12 protons). Another 10 percent is Mg-25, and still another 11 percent is Mg-26. The other known isotopes are artificially produced by bombarding the atoms with neutrons. These isotopes are radioactive, meaning they emit energetic particles. They are magnesium-20, -21, -22, -23, and Mg-27 through -31.

# OUT OF THE EARTH

The oceans of the young Earth were rich in potassium and magnesium. This is no longer the case, but the presence of these elements is known because they exist in major quantities in the rocks of Earth's crust. They also exist in all living things.

More than 60 minerals found in Earth's crust contain magnesium. By weight, magnesium makes up 2.5 percent of the crust. By volume, it is 0.3 percent of the crust. Magnesium is the seventh most abundant element.

When the Soviet Union sent a Venera spacecraft to the surface of the planet Venus in 1970, the craft carried instruments to detect and measure the amount of various elements making up the planetary surface. Magnesium was among the elements that were measured and found to

:HEPA-9  22.10.197

The Soviet Union's Venera spacecraft discovered that magnesium is one of the elements on the surface of Venus.

14

exist on Venus in about the same amounts as on Earth. Mars, too, contains considerable magnesium. Clearly, it is an important element in the rocks of the solar system.

## Dolomite

Dolomite is a type of mineral that existed first as limestone, or calcium carbonate, $CaCO_3$. (Carbon is C, element #6.) Soon after this calcium rock was formed, the calcium content was exchanged for magnesium, making $MgCO_3$. The process releases calcium ions into the water. This exchange probably took place in an ancient sea.

**Crystals of dolomite mineral are seen here embedded in dolomite rock, which is also called dolostone.**

Rocks made up of this combination of magnesium carbonate and calcium carbonate minerals are often called dolomite. Because of the ease with which the rock can be confused with the mineral, dolomite rock is sometimes called dolostone. It is a sedimentary rock, calcium magnesium carbonate, $CaMg(CO_3)_2$. It was formed when the calcium-carbonate-containing shells of marine animals sank to the seafloor and were compressed.

Dolomite was named for the mountains where it was first studied. The Dolomite Mountains, which are part of the Alps in northeastern Italy, were named for the eighteenth-century French geologist Dieudonné Dolomieu.

A mineral called periclase is magnesium oxide, MgO, which appears as rounded granules in marble, an important building stone. Periclase is dolomite that has been transformed at some time in the past by high temperatures.

## Mining Magnesium

The main mineral source of magnesium in the United States is the ore magnesite, which is really another type of magnesium carbonate, $MgCO_3$. It is mined primarily in Clark County, Nevada.

Magnesium metal is extracted from dolomite by a process called thermal reduction. Crushed rock is heated until it breaks into magnesium oxide and calcium oxide, giving off extra carbon dioxide.

$$CaMg(CO_3)_2 + heat \rightarrow CaO + MgO + 2CO_2$$

The carbon dioxide is driven off, and silicon is added to the mix. With sufficient heat added, the magnesium vaporizes and can be condensed to metal. A rock slag remains:

$$2CaO + 2MgO + Si + heat \rightarrow 2Mg + Ca_2SiO_4$$

The molten metal is poured into ingots, or brick shapes, and sent to manufacturers for use in various products.

## The Softest Mineral

Other magnesium minerals are also useful. One of them is the softest mineral known, called talc, $Mg_3Si_4O_{10}(OH)_2$. Talc is often found with magnesite and dolomite. This magnesium silicate mineral is at the very bottom of the Mohs Hardness Scale. Created by German geologist Friedrich Mohs, the scale easily gives an indication of the hardness of a mineral by what scratches it—and by what it scratches.

On his scale, Mohs gave diamond a 10, indicating the highest level of hardness, because it scratches everything and nothing can scratch it. Talc is 1, at the softest level. It will not scratch anything it touches, but everything can mark or scratch talc.

Talc powders easily and feels greasy However, it can be found in compact masses called soapstone. Soapstone has long

The magnesium mineral called talc is so soft that it can be scratched with a fingernail.

## Mohs Hardness Scale

**1 talc:** easily scratched by a fingernail
**2 gypsum:** harder to scratch with a fingernail than talc but can be done
**3 calcite:** very easily scratched with a knife
**4 fluorite:** not quite as easily scratched by a knife
**5 apatite:** scratched by a knife but only with difficulty
**6 orthoclase:** a knife will not scratch it but it will scratch glass
**7 quartz:** easily scratches glass
**8 topaz:** very easily scratches glass
**9 corundum:** can cut glass
**10 diamond:** easily cuts glass and is used as a glass cutter; scratches all other minerals

been used as a stone for carving. Ancient Egyptians used soapstone for many of their scarabs, which were carved beetles, symbolizing the rebirth of the sun and life. Today, talc is used as the powder that holds color for face powder. When perfumed, it becomes talcum powder, for use after baths. Both talc and magnesium carbonate ($MgCO_3$) are sometimes used as the abrasive (the rough material) in toothpaste and tooth powder.

Chrysotile is a fibrous form of the magnesium mineral serpentine. It can be compressed for use as fireproofing.

# Serpentine Asbestos

Serpentine is a magnesium-and-silicon mineral that looks roughly mottled, as if it were a serpent's skin. Regular crystalline serpentine does not have many uses. However, a fibrous (hair-like) form of serpentine, known as chrysotile, is the most common variety of asbestos. Asbestos is one of several different fibrous natural minerals that is used in fireproofing because it does not burn or melt. It is often used to wrap furnace pipes and provide insulation in the ceilings of schools and other public buildings.

Some years ago, asbestos acquired a bad reputation because it was found that asbestos workers had an extraordinarily high rate of cancer and other lung diseases. The long-used insulation came to be regarded as carcinogenic, or cancer-causing. Numerous schools were found to have asbestos insulation, and many of them had to spend a great deal of money having such insulation replaced. Some buildings were shut down. But it turned out that chrysotile was not the culprit. Instead, it was another variety of asbestos, known as amphibole asbestos. All major nations except the United States are again allowing chrysotile to be used in building.

A company in Canada is attempting to rescue magnesium from a closed asbestos mine. It is processing the tailings, or left-over materials, for the magnesium contained in them.

## Sulfates and Silicates

The mineral magnesium sulfate, $MgSO_4$, was first separated out of the waters of Epsom. Interestingly, the mineral comes in several varieties, depending on how many water molecules are attached to the magnesium sulfate molecule. The mineral kieserite is $MgSO_4 \cdot H_2O$. It is found in brine that has evaporated. If kieserite is allowed to stand in the open air, it absorbs more water vapor from the air, turning into epsomite, $MgSO_4 \cdot 7H_2O$. If some of the water evaporates from epsomite, it turns into hexahydrate, $MgSO_4 \cdot 6H_2O$.

A collector in Arizona holds a sample of a meteorite, a rock from outer space. Special lighting reveals the chunks of olivine contained in the rock.

There are many kinds of silicate (containing silicon and oxygen) minerals called olivine, but the name of this group of minerals comes from the magnesium-bearing one that is yellow-green. Geologists believe that olivines are the main mineral found in Earth's mantle. That is the region of molten rock below the crust and above the core. Rocks containing olivines are igneous rocks—they were formed from molten rock that came to the Earth's surface and hardened. One variety of olivine is fosterite, $Mg_2SiO_4$, which, when clear and unblemished, is a deep yellow-green gemstone called peridot.

Huge expanses of olivine have been found on Mars too. Because it had not been greatly weathered—worn away by water and heat—scientists have recently determined that throughout most of its history, Mars was cold and dry. This discovery disappointed science-fiction writers who had written of a wet, warm, junglelike period in Martian history.

## Minerals in Water

We tend to think of water as just plain $H_2O$, molecules consisting of two atoms of hydrogen and one of oxygen. But water in nature contains many other molecules, especially those of minerals dissolved in it. They were dissolved by rainwater from rocks and soil and carried into the water. The dissolved magnesium in water is a cation (positive ion), $Mg^{2+}$.

Ions are carried into freshwater supplies, both on Earth's surface—in lakes and rivers—and through the soil into the groundwater. On their way through the soil, magnesium ions can become part of the soil, where plants absorb them through their roots. It's estimated that 1 acre (0.4 hectare) of topsoil can contain between 3,600 and 12,000 kilograms (8,000 to 26,000 pounds) of magnesium.

Eventually, though, almost all water makes its way to the ocean, and the various minerals that have been picked up along the way accumulate there. The chloride ion, $Cl^-$, is the most common, followed by the sodium ion, $Na^+$. They are drawn to each other, forming electrically balanced sodium chloride, NaCl. It is NaCl that gives ocean water the taste of salt.

Magnesium is the third most common ion, making up about 1.3 grams per kilogram of seawater. That adds up to 0.13 percent of seawater. The magnesium ions, too, attach themselves to chloride ions, making magnesium chloride, $MgCl_2$. It is as magnesium chloride that magnesium is extracted from seawater.

Actually, minerals are rarely obtained directly from water

The huge electrolysis machines used today to obtain metallic magnesium from brine contain many electrodes. Even so, the devices work just as Humphry Davy's simple laboratory electrolysis equipment did.

taken from the sea. Instead, the substance called brine is used. Some pockets of ancient seawater remained when the seas evaporated. These pockets never completely evaporated but turned into deposits of mushy salts—brine. Brines can often be just pumped out of the earth for processing. Table salt is often obtained from brines, along with other minerals.

## The Dow Process

The most common process for obtaining metals from seawater is called the Dow process. It was invented by Herbert Dow, founder of the Dow Chemical Company, in about 1895. Dow figured out how to obtain a number of elements from the brine deposits located beneath Midland, Michigan. He managed to produce bromine (Br, element #35), then chlorine, iodine (I, #53), sodium, and then magnesium from brine. The Dow process uses electrolysis, the same process Sir Humphry Davy used 200 years ago. Dow did not stop producing magnesium until the late 1990s, when their largest plant, which was in Texas, was destroyed by storms.

In the Dow process, crushed dolomite, $CaMg(CO_3)_2$, is mixed with brine. The magnesium chloride in the brine combines with magnesium and calcium to form magnesium hydroxide, $Mg(OH)_2$, and calcium chloride, $CaCl_2$. When the magnesium hydroxide precipitates (forms a solid material that settles out), it is pumped into another chamber. There it is mixed with hydrochloric acid, HCl, and the magnesium hydroxide forms magnesium chloride and water. Most of the water is evaporated, leaving purer magnesium chloride than existed at the start of the process. It is then electrolyzed to obtain a metal that is 99.9 percent pure. In its molten state, the metal is poured into molds for shipment to manufacturers.

## Hard Water

The same ions—especially magnesium and calcium—that make ocean water salty can remain in the freshwater supplies of our planet. Such water is called hard water. You know whether or not you have hard water by how well your soap lathers when you wash. If your soap doesn't produce much suds, you are washing with hard water.

The minerals that make water hard can accumulate in a coffee pot or a flower vase if water is allowed to remain unchanged for a long period of time. Most people periodically clean coffee pots or vases with vinegar, which dissolves the mineral deposit.

When used for washing clothes, regular soap can leave a scum on the clothing that is formed by the minerals in the water. This residue is strictly a chemical reaction between the soap and the minerals. Modern detergents were invented to prevent this scum from forming in hard water.

Mineral compounds in hard water tend to accumulate in the pipes of a house's plumbing system. Eventually, so much of this material, called scale, can build up that it plugs up the system. If something is not done about the hard water, the pipes may have to be replaced. However, there are now systems that clear scale electronically.

It is easier and cheaper to make hard water soft. This is done with a water softener. The method most often used today is called ion exchange. The minerals in water are in the form of ions, so the softener just exchanges magnesium ions, $Mg^{2+}$, and calcium ions, $Ca^{2+}$, for another kind, usually sodium, $Na^+$.

Bead-like substances called resins in the softener allow ion exchange to take place on their surfaces. During normal use, the hard water containing $Ca^{2+}$ and $Mg^{2+}$ ions enters the resin. These ions will exchange for Na+ ions and the magnesium and calcium ions will be left on the resin. The water—now "softened"—contains only $Na^+$ ions. Softened water flows out from the tank to the kitchen and bathroom of the house.

After several days, the resin is full of calcium and magnesium ions and needs to be regenerated. $Na^+$ ions from the brine tank will force the other ions off the resin. They are washed down the drain and the softener returns to normal use. The salt pellets are gradually used up and have to be replenished occasionally.

**A home water softener removes minerals such as magnesium by exchanging ions with salt.**

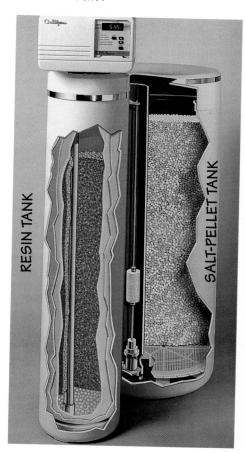

RESIN TANK

SALT-PELLET TANK

# AT THE HEART OF GREEN

Much of the natural world appears green. This is because most of the plants around us are green. Why green? Could it just as easily have been purple or orange? Perhaps, but most of Earth's plants contain one very special molecule called chlorophyll. And chlorophyll is green. In fact, the word *chlorophyll* means "green leaf."

Just about all animals on Earth depend on plants for their food. Even the meat-eaters eat animals that have eaten plants. But very few plants eat animals (there are a few plants that suck juices out of insects). Instead, plants depend on chlorophyll for their food. This molecule has the seemingly magical ability to convert energy from sunlight, and carbon dioxide from the air, and water from the ground into food that gives the plant the energy to carry on its life processes.

This making of food by a plant's

Ireland has been said to have "forty shades of green"—and they all come from the chlorophyll molecule, which contains magnesium.

chlorophyll is called photosynthesis, which means "putting together with light." The reaction of carbon dioxide and water in the presence of sunlight produces simple sugar plus oxygen (which animals breathe).

$$6CO_2 + 12H_2O + \text{sunlight} \rightarrow C_6H_{12}O_6 + 6O_2 + 6H_2O$$

But the reaction is anything but simple. Many different reactions happen within the plant to make the sugar form. It took scientists many decades to sort it all out.

## Investigating Greenness

In 1817, two French pharmacists, Pierre Pelletier and Joseph Caventou, were looking for natural substances that could be used as medicines. They isolated numerous important substances from plants, such as strychnine (a poison) and caffeine (a stimulant). But for the most important substance they found, they could see no immediate use. It was the basic green matter in plants, which they named chlorophyll.

Step by step, scientists added to the knowledge of chlorophyll and plant nutrition in general. German botanist Julius von Sachs showed in 1865 that the substance was located in separate slipper-shaped bodies within plant cells. These bodies were later named chloroplasts.

Richard Willstätter was a German chemist who worked in Switzerland in the early part of the twentieth century. In 1913, he showed that magnesium atoms are present in chlorophyll. He also showed that chlorophyll is very similar in structure to heme, which is part of hemoglobin, the substance in red blood cells that carries oxygen. Willstätter was awarded the 1915 Nobel Prize in chemistry. In the 1920s, another German chemist, Hans Fischer, refined Willstätter's work and won another Nobel Prize.

Further details about how photosynthesis actually works had to wait for American biochemist Melvin Calvin in the 1950s. He

**Dr. Melvin Calvin won his 1961 Nobel Prize for his investigation into the workings of photosynthesis in plants.**

and his colleagues at the University of California at Berkeley used radioactive carbon dioxide to trace and describe all the complex biochemical events that occur in photosynthesis. He found almost two dozen enzymes involved in these events. Obviously, photosynthesis is not so simple a process after all. Calvin, too, won a Nobel Prize, in 1961, for his work on this most fundamental activity of life.

Finally, in 1965, Robert Burns Woodward of Harvard University won a Nobel Prize for synthesizing, or putting together out of laboratory ingredients, a number of different complex molecules, including chlorophyll. He was able to build on all the important scientific research that had gone on before him.

## The Magic Molecule

These inquisitive scientists found out that the heart of a chlorophyll molecule is a magnesium ion, $Mg^{2+}$. This ion is surrounded by what is called a porphyrin ring, a circle of molecules containing nitrogen (N, element #7) and carbon. A long chain of carbon and hydrogen atoms is attached at one side of the ring.

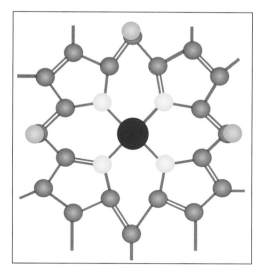

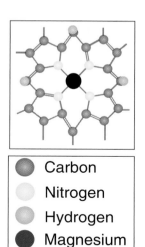

The center of the chlorophyll molecule (left) is a magnesium ion surrounded by a porphyrin ring. It is almost identical to the oxygen-carrying heme molecule of humans (right), which has iron at its center.

| | |
|---|---|
| ● | Carbon |
| ○ | Nitrogen |
| ○ | Hydrogen |
| ● | Magnesium |
| ● | Iron |

As researchers discovered, this structure is the same as the heme in animal blood, except that instead of having a magnesium ion at its center, heme has an iron (Fe, for *ferrum,* element #26) ion there. In addition to being the red substance in blood, hemoglobin is responsible for the red color on the combs and wattles of chickens. Combs are the red, fleshy growths that stand up from a chicken's head, and wattles are those that hang from its chin.

The structure of a metal atom surrounded by a ring of non-metallic atoms is called a coordination compound. Coordination compounds frequently show up as color in chemicals. In heme, they are bright-red. In chlorophyll, they are green. They also occur in green bird feathers. Sometimes porphyrins combine with copper to produce deep-red feathers.

## Within the Chloroplasts

There are actually two different kinds of chlorophyll pigments in higher plants. They are called *chlorophyll a* and

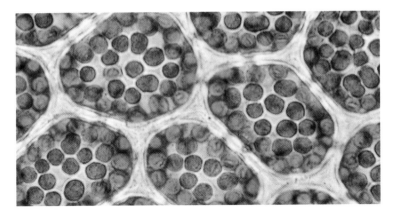

Chlorophyll is produced within the chloroplasts, small bodies within the cells of green plant tissue.

*chlorophyll b.* The magnesium ion and porphyrin ring are the same in both kinds of chlorophyll, but they vary in the structure of the side chain. Both kinds of chlorophyll absorb sunlight, but they absorb different portions of the sun's radiation. The *a* form of chlorophyll is considerably more abundant than *b.*

Some other pigments, such as the yellow and red pigments called carotenoids, help with photosynthesis by absorbing sunlight and sending it to the chlorophyll. During most of the year, these other pigments are overwhelmed by the green pigments of chlorophyll. They become visible in the fall after the chlorophyll in the green leaves of deciduous trees starts to decompose.

The single-celled organisms called blue-green bacteria used to be regarded as a type of algae because there is chlorophyll in the single cell. However, the molecule is not isolated in chloroplasts. Instead, the coloring matter is spread throughout the cell. The green mixes with a blue pigment that makes the bacteria blue-green.

## Making and Using Food

The basic foods produced by photosynthesis are carbohydrates, molecules made up of carbon and water atoms (two hydrogens and one oxygen). Carbohydrates are sugars and starches (many sugar molecules linked together).

Within every cell—both plant and animal—are molecules called ATP, for adenosine triphosphate. When a cell requires energy to burn, the ATP molecules split apart, releasing energy. In chlorophyll, they transfer their energy to a sugar molecule, where it is used to hold the molecule together.

When the plant needs energy to carry out its other processes, oxygen atoms link up with the sugar molecules. This is combustion, or burning, of the sugar molecule, which releases energy. When plants or plant products are eaten by animals, the same thing happens. The plant tissues are digested and sugars in them become part of the animal cells. In animal cells, the sugar is burned for energy.

A chemist measures the natural fluorescence of chlorophyll in an orange tree to determine the health of the tree.

## The Need for Magnesium

Clearly, green plants cannot grow or repair themselves without the chemicals to make new supplies of chlorophyll. Magnesium is one of those chemicals.

Magnesium is not one of the nutrients that standard fertilizers provide. A plant grower—whether of house plants or crops—must keep an eye out for possible magnesium deficiency and take the necessary steps to treat it. Corn, for example, requires considerable magnesium in its soil. Rice requires almost none. Grapevines greatly benefit from the

Corn requires a great deal of magnesium. Under special lights, the plants in front show that they are deficient in magnesium by their lighter color.

application of magnesium to the soil they grow in.

Without enough magnesium in a plant's soil, photosynthesis does not take place at the rate needed to maintain plant growth and cell replacement. The magnesium that is available moves to the areas where new leaves are growing rapidly. That means that the older leaves are the first to show a magnesium deficiency. Unfortunately, when a plant lacks magnesium, it may seem to a plant grower that it has had too much calcium because the symptoms are the same.

Soils that contain less than 100 parts per million (ppm) of magnesium are generally considered deficient. The soil that contains the least natural magnesium is usually acidic and sandy, although soil that has been treated with too much potassium can lose its magnesium.

Always using softened water on plants can gradually lead to a magnesium and calcium deficiency. People with water softeners in their houses can avoid the problem by leaving one water pipe unconnected to the softener. This way, some untreated water is available.

Garden soils and the soil in potted plants can be treated by mixing crushed dolomite into the soil. On a smaller scale, Epsom salts can also be applied, about one tablespoon dissolved in 1 liter (1 quart) of water.

Magnesium deficiency appears as chlorosis, meaning that the strong green color of a healthy plant gradually disappears, from the outer edges of the leaves inward to the main vein. The leaves may gradually become a strong bronze color, which has led to magnesium deficiency being called bronzing disease.

## First They Have to Eat It

Animals that chew a cud—such as cattle, sheep, and goats—sometimes develop a serious condition called grass tetany, which can lead to paralysis and death. It results from too little magnesium in the grass they eat. Agricultural scientists have developed a new kind of hardy grass of the variety called tall fescue, which is common to pastureland. The new one, with the trade name HiMag, contains considerably more magnesium than other grasses. Apparently the animals find it delicious.

Grass tetany can occur when animals eat grasses that have been fertilized with too much potassium. In the four stomachs of these animals, potassium, rather than magnesium, is absorbed. Even if the animal obtains magnesium from the grass, it is not absorbed during digestion. Adding more magnesium to the grass helps prevent the condition.

A scientist from the U.S. Department of Agriculture inspects a test field of a high-magnesium grass that will help prevent grass tetany, a serious disease in livestock.

# THE CRITICAL ION

In 1859, researchers discovered magnesium ions in the bodies of humans. Naturally, they began to investigate the function of these ions. In the 1920s, magnesium was determined by scientists to be essential to animal life. It was another 30 years before researchers discovered that a magnesium deficiency can be harmful to human health. They found that magnesium is an essential element, a macronutrient, one needed in fairly large quantities. It was the last of the eleven macronutrients to be confirmed.

Magnesium exists in the body as an electrolyte, or ion, $Mg^{2+}$. It plays a secondary role in many bodily functions and processes, which does not mean that it is less than essential. Magnesium is secondary to calcium in bones and teeth and it is secondary to

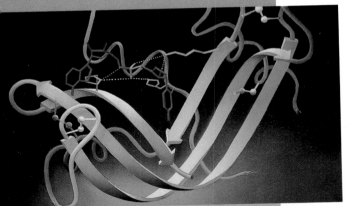

Magnesium ions are found in every cell of the body, where they are involved in the manufacture of DNA and RNA. This computer model shows RNA.

potassium in regulating fluid activities within cells. But neither of those other elements will work properly if magnesium is not present in sufficient quantities.

Magnesium is present in every cell of the body because every cell contains DNA (deoxyribonucleic acid) and RNA (ribonucleic acid). These complex substances control the genes. Magnesium plays a role in the continuous synthesis of the many ingredients in these substances. It also is necessary whenever a cell uses or stores energy, which, of course, is most of the time.

There are about 25 grams (1 ounce) of magnesium in the human body at any one time. About half of that is found in the bones. The remainder is contained primarily in the fluid within cells. There is still considerable mystery as to just how magnesium functions in the cells. Methods of studying these intricate activities have not yet been found. But it is clear that magnesium plays an essential role in many activities that keep us alive.

## In the Digestive System

Magnesium can play a role in digestion, both at the beginning of the process and at the end. At the beginning, it is often used as an antacid. The stomach produces an acid called hydrochloric acid, HCl, which aids digestion. However, in some people, this acid can back up in the esophagus (the lower end of the throat) and be painful. This discomfort is called heartburn.

To relieve heartburn, people swallow various compounds called antacids because they turn the acid to a neutral substance. One common antacid is milk of magnesia—a suspension of powdered magnesium hydroxide, $Mg(OH)_2$. "Suspension" means that the powder does not actually dissolve. Instead, it settles to the bottom of the bottle, which should be shaken before taking the antacid. In the stomach, the antacid combines with hydrogen ions from hydrochloric acid to create magnesium ions and water, reducing the acidity of the stomach.

Sunlight is good for health because it produces vitamin D. Too much sunlight, though, can be harmful.

At the other end of the digestive system, milk of magnesia works as a laxative. The chemical makes a person who is constipated have a bowel movement. Any magnesium product taken in excess does this.

In between, magnesium in food has to be absorbed, or the ions will not reach the bones and cells. Only about one-third of the magnesium in our food is actually absorbed by the body. And without adequate supplies of vitamin D, even that one-third cannot be adequately absorbed. Often called the sunshine vitamin, vitamin D is produced in our skin when it is exposed to sunlight. Because people in northern countries often do not produce enough natural vitamin D, it is added to milk. This vitamin is equally important in the absorption of calcium for building bones.

The kidneys, which control the manufacture and output of urine, play a vital role in the balance of magnesium in the body. Normally, two-thirds of the magnesium we take in is excreted in the urine, without ever really being absorbed for use in the body. However, if a person is not getting enough magnesium, the kidneys halt the excretion of magnesium and send the ions into the bloodstream to travel where they are needed.

This recycling of magnesium by the kidneys is one reason

that doctors often do not know when a person has a magnesium deficiency. The work of the kidneys can hide the deficiency for quite a while, until the body itself begins to reveal it.

## In the Bones

The bones act as a storage cabinet for magnesium. They are made primarily of calcium and phosphorus (P, element #15), but ions of magnesium and sodium are stored within bone tissue. Some magnesium ions in bone are bound to phosphate, making the molecule $Mg_3(PO_4)_2$. The rest of the ions are free to move to wherever they are needed in the body.

A great deal of publicity has been given to the importance of calcium in preventing the disease called osteoporosis. This is a loss of bone density, resulting in bone becoming thin and breaking easily. Although this disease may not show its dangerous effects until later in life, doctors now know that preventing it from happening at all depends on people obtaining the right nutrients from childhood.

Calcium alone will not do the job. For strong bones, a person needs to also get enough magnesium to make calcium bind into bones and teeth properly. The amount of magnesium needed is about half the amount of calcium.

## Magnesium the Activator

Magnesium ions are just one of several different kinds of ions, called electrolytes, needed in the body. Inside cells, magnesium ions are second in quantity only to potassium ions. Their presence within the cell is required in adequate amounts for the other electrolytes (sodium, potassium, chloride, and phosphate) to work. Magnesium ions within cells have been found to be involved in so many different functions that magnesium has been called a "chronic regulator," meaning it keeps the normal function of the cell going.

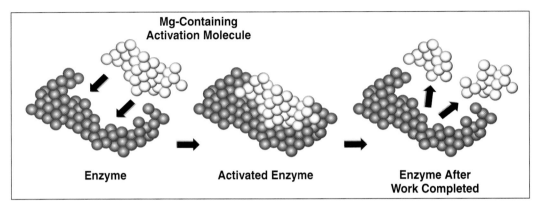

Mg-Containing
Activation Molecule

Enzyme          Activated Enzyme          Enzyme After
Work Completed

It is estimated that at least 300 enzymes require magnesium
as a catalyst to activate them. After the enzymes do their work,
the magnesium-containing molecule, or co-enzyme, separates.

One of magnesium's functions is to activate enzymes. Enzymes are organic catalysts, which means they are substances that cause other substances to do their jobs. Catalysts are not permanently changed by the process.

Without magnesium to activate it, any enzyme involving phosphorus will not do its job. And phosphorus is an essential part of the life-giving molecule adenosine triphosphate, or ATP. ATP is the source of biological energy. This is the same ATP molecule found in plants. The sugar molecule produced in plants must be broken down in the cells for cellular functions to occur. Enzymes prompted by magnesium ions make this happen.

Magnesium's role in ATP is only one of many functions it performs within the body. Magnesium ions travel in the blood to where they are needed. They are most concentrated in the tissues that are busiest. These are in the brain, heart, liver, and kidneys. The cells of these organs are the most active and use the most energy.

## In the Blood

The body requires a continuous supply—although a very small one—of magnesium ions in blood plasma. Plasma is the clear fluid in which blood cells move. The amount of magnesium in blood is controlled by the parathyroid gland, which is located behind the thyroid gland in the neck. The parathyroid gland secretes a chemical called parathyroid hormone. It regulates the use of calcium by the body.

When the amount of $Mg^{2+}$ ions in blood plasma drops, the change causes the parathyroid gland to secrete parathyroid hormone. The presence of this hormone in the blood prompts magnesium stored in bone to leave the bone and go where it is needed.

Not all the magnesium ions in blood plasma are free to move wherever they are needed, however. About one-third of them are bound to a blood protein called albumin. Albumin is responsible for keeping ions moving from capillaries (the very tiniest blood vessels) into cells.

A deficiency of magnesium is difficult to detect because essential elements are usually measured in blood tests. But because both the kidneys and the bones supply magnesium as needed by the blood, deficiency does not immediately reveal itself. Long after it has started to cause problems, the deficiency will show up in special blood tests.

## Magnesium versus Calcium

Clearly, the roles of magnesium and calcium in the body are intertwined. Both are required, and one does not work properly without the other. Sometimes they work together. Sometimes they oppose each other, but the absence or shortage of one affects the efficiency of the other.

Calcium ions stimulate muscle fibers to contract (tighten or close). Magnesium ions make them return to their normal state, or relax. Calcium ions make blood vessels contract. Magnesium ions make them relax again.

When the blood plasma does not contain as much magnesium as it should, nerve and muscle cells are in a constant state of stimulation, in which they are continuously contracting without ever fully relaxing. The person becomes irritable and nervous, and the muscles may have small continuous tremors.

The relaxing effect of magnesium can be important in the condition called asthma. Asthma is a swelling of the breathing passages, brought on by allergies, stress, or a variety of other causes, making it difficult for the person to breathe in enough air. Doses of magnesium make the smooth muscles that control the airways relax. A large dose of magnesium directly into a vein can stop an asthma attack immediately. However, giving a person with asthma regular doses of magnesium does not appear to prevent attacks.

If a person gets too much magnesium, its ability to make tissues relax can put a person to sleep. This is one reason why kidney failure makes a person gradually fall into unconsciousness—the kidneys are no longer eliminating magnesium from the body, and the ions accumulate.

## Diabetes

Glucose—sometimes called blood sugar—is the basic chemical resulting from the digestion of the foods we eat. It is the same simple sugar produced by photosynthesis in plants, $C_6H_{12}O_6$. Glucose is the form in which food reaches the individual cells of the body, where it is used for energy.

The level of glucose in the blood has to be kept fairly even for the body to remain healthy. The job of keeping glucose at the proper level, regardless of what we eat, belongs to a substance called insulin. Insulin is produced in the pancreas, a

A girl with Type I diabetes removes a container of insulin from her refrigerator. A daily injection of the insulin keeps her healthy.

gland located at the top of the small intestine.

Diabetes is a disease that destroys the insulin-producing cells in the pancreas. Without insulin, the body, in effect, starves itself to death because the sugar it needs for energy does not get transported from the blood into the cells.

People with diabetes have a low level of magnesium ions in their blood. If there is not enough magnesium in the body, insulin fails to work properly in controlling blood-sugar levels. No one is sure yet whether a person with diabetes develops a magnesium deficiency or whether a magnesium deficiency plays a role in the development of diabetes. But the results of a major study that were reported in 1997 indicated that people who had a low level of magnesium in their blood were twice as likely later to develop diabetes as someone with a high level. However, the finding did not seem to apply to people of African heritage, who are affected with diabetes at an extremely high rate.

The kind of diabetes that may start in childhood is called Type 1 diabetes or insulin-dependent diabetes. The pancreas never produces enough insulin for the body's needs. A person with this condition may need to take insulin all his or her life.

Type 2 diabetes, also called non-insulin-dependent diabetes, occurs when the cells stop reacting to the insulin they receive.

This kind of diabetes often develops in overweight adults. It has recently been found that this kind of diabetes may also occur when a person doesn't have enough magnesium in the body.

## Blood Pressure

People with diabetes sometimes develop clots, or clumpy substances, in their blood, as do many other people for many other reasons. If a clot forms in the vessels leading to the heart, it can stop oxygen from reaching the heart, causing a heart attack, or cardiac arrest. If a clot forms in a blood vessel in the brain, it can cause what is called a stroke. A stroke can do permanent damage to the function of the nerves in the body, leaving a person unable to walk or talk properly.

Both of these problems can be caused by the condition called high blood pressure, or hypertension. Blood pressure is the force blood exerts against the walls of the arteries, which are the blood vessels that carry oxygen-rich blood from the lungs to the body. In someone with high blood pressure, the heart has to work too hard to keep blood flowing. It may be caused by

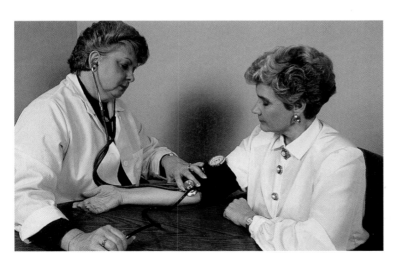

This woman's blood pressure is being measured. If the pressure is higher than is healthy, she will probably be given medicines that will make fluid leave her body.

atherosclerosis, a condition in which the arteries become plugged up with a fatty substance called cholesterol.

What role does magnesium play in these conditions? In a study of men with high blood pressure, those who received the most magnesium (about 450 milligrams each day) had one-third fewer incidents of heart problems than those who received the least (typically 245 mg a day). Similarly, in areas where there is little magnesium in the water, the incidence of heart disease is higher than elsewhere. Some researchers think that the single most important thing people can do to prevent heart attacks and strokes is to get an adequate amount of magnesium.

## In the Brain

The brain sends signals to the body to carry out various activities. These can be as conscious as choosing to move the legs to run. They can be as automatic—and unconscious—as signaling the heart to beat faster when running.

Such signals are electrical. They consist of a change in ion concentration that originates in the brain and moves through the

**A spinal tap is a procedure in which cerebrospinal fluid is removed from the spinal cord and analyzed.**

spinal cord, which is located within the vertebrae, or backbone. Nerves branch from the spinal cord throughout the body.

Both the brain and the spinal cord—the centers of what is called the central nervous system—have spaces through which flows an important fluid called the cerebrospinal fluid. This colorless fluid contains more magnesium ions than anywhere else in the body. It cushions the brain and spinal cord from impact. It also provides an environment through which flow the ions, including magnesium, that make the nervous system function.

When the central nervous system is injured (which can be the result of anything from a blow to a stroke to ingesting a poison), the amount of magnesium ions in the fluid is reduced. Studies are being made to see if administering magnesium sulfate or magnesium chloride after an injury may speed the recovery of nervous system tissue.

Terrible headaches called migraines may stem from a lack of magnesium in the system. This relationship is not yet certain. Migraines are headaches that follow a specific pattern in an individual and may last a long time, even days, unless something can stop them when they first begin. Doses of magnesium have been shown to reduce the severity and the duration of migraines, probably by keeping the blood vessels from spasming.

## Not Enough Magnesium

Alcohol, stress, cocaine, caffeine, asthma medicines, cola drinks (which are high in phosphates), and too much dietary fat are among the reasons that a person could develop a magnesium deficiency. The amount of magnesium in the body can also be reduced by using diuretics (water pills). Diuretics are often prescribed by doctors to treat high blood pressure, because they reduce the volume of blood that moves through blood vessels. The water leaves the body as urine, but so, too, do potassium and magnesium. Both of these elements need to be replaced.

Of all drugs responsible for deficiencies of magnesium, alcohol is known to be the worst. It causes the kidneys to excrete more magnesium than they usually do. Alcohol itself, in large amounts, is known to cause high blood pressure, stroke, and sudden death. Such tragedies may happen because of a serious deficiency in magnesium brought about by drinking alcohol.

The most obvious first symptom of magnesium deficiency is an irregular heart rhythm. Muscle weakness, mental confusion, and listlessness can follow. Long-term deficiency may play a role in the development of diabetes and osteoporosis and many other conditions, including memory loss.

## Daily Requirements

Traditionally, the recommended daily dosage of magnesium has been 250 to 350 milligrams. However, in recent years, it has become clear that more magnesium is needed than formerly thought. In 1999, the National Academy of Sciences established new recommendations. They say that women over age 30 should get at least 320 milligrams of magnesium daily, while men over 30 should consume at least 420 milligrams daily. A teenage girl should get 360 milligrams, and a teenage boy needs 410 milligrams.

In the nineteenth century, people ate more unprocessed foods, such as whole-grain bread, than we do today. When wheat is milled to make white flour, an estimated 85 percent of the magnesium in the wheat grain is lost. The figure is

**Wheat that has not been refined contains more magnesium than milled flour does.**

These women are boiling raw sugar to make a thick dark syrup called molasses. It is very high in magnesium.

even more stunning with refined sugar. The refining process removes all but 2 percent of the magnesium. That's why molasses, which is the fluid left over from the sugar-refining process, is so high in magnesium.

When people ate more of such foods, they took in 475 to 500 milligrams of magnesium each day. Today, primarily because of food processing, people tend to get only between 140 and 265 milligrams from their daily diet.

Good natural sources of magnesium are legumes (dried beans of various kinds), dark green vegetables such as broccoli and spinach, grains (especially high-fiber cereals) and nuts (especially almonds and cashews). Bananas and orange juice, which are excellent sources of potassium, are also high in magnesium, although most other common fruits are not. The fish with the highest magnesium content is halibut. Fortunately, fresh water also contains magnesium, especially hard water. And— good news!—a single 113-gram (4-ounce) chocolate bar contains 55 milligrams of magnesium.

Scientists have not yet achieved a complete understanding of the role of magnesium within the cells of the human body. Although the overall amount of magnesium in the body is not large, taken together, the total effect of all of magnesium's functions gives it great importance.

# THE METAL AND INDUSTRY

Magnesium is a silvery-white, shiny metal. It is the lightest metal that can be formed or molded by machines into different shapes. It is the fifth most abundant metal in Earth's crust after aluminum (Al, element #13), iron, calcium, and sodium. In weight, it is one-third lighter than aluminum, and thus has become important in airplanes and spacecraft.

Magnesium is very malleable, meaning that it can be worked, or manipulated, easily. It retains this characteristic when it is used in an alloy. Alloys are just mixtures, not chemical reactions, but they can change the character of the materials being mixed together. When magnesium is added to aluminum, for example, it makes the aluminum easier to shape, roll, or work with a machine.

Metal ladders made of an alloy of

**Homeowners often use ladders made of aluminum and magnesium because they are lightweight and strong.**

aluminum-magnesium alloy are stronger and lighter than those made solely of aluminum. As early as the first Mariner flights to other planets, spacecraft have had magnesium frames. Magnesium metal is being used in lightweight mobile computers to provide strength (and protect data). Also, many brands of luggage use magnesium metal for the rigid frames.

## Twentieth-Century Alloys

In choosing an alloy, manufacturers decide what traits they need most. The main benefit of magnesium is its lightness, but it is also soft, so something has to be added to make it sturdier. It gains strength from the addition of aluminum and zinc (Zn, element #30), which make it easier to mold into formed parts. Magnesium gains corrosion resistance from manganese (Mn, #25). The addition of thorium (Th, #90) lets magnesium be used at higher temperatures.

An alloy called magnalium is only 5 percent magnesium with 95 percent aluminum. It is often used for medical instruments. Other alloys containing a greater percentage of magnesium have also been given the name *magnalium* by the pyrotechnics, or fireworks, industry.

Another variety of alloy that contains much more magnesium than aluminum, as well as something else such as zinc or manganese, is known as Dowmetal. The first Dowmetal was developed by the Dow Chemical Company just after World War I (1914–1919). It contained 93.5 percent magnesium, 6 percent aluminum, and 0.5 percent manganese. In 1921, the famous Indianapolis 500 auto race was won by Tommy Milton, who was driving a car that had Dowmetal pistons in the engine.

## Using Magnesium's Qualities

More than half of all magnesium compounds used in the United States are in refractories. A refractory is a metallic material

Jean and Auguste Piccard pose with the Dowmetal sphere that protected them on their balloon ascent of 16,765 meters (55,000 feet) into the stratosphere in 1932.

that can withstand high temperatures or harsh chemicals. One of the prime uses of refractory products today is to line the huge cylinders in which petroleum is cracked, or broken into its component parts. It is also used in small furnaces where special metallurgical processes are carried out.

Magnesium oxide, MgO, is used to line the furnace in the open-hearth process of producing steel, as well as in the manufacture of glass and cement. It also absorbs waste chemicals during water-treatment processes.

Magnesium readily combines with sulfur, which is an impurity in most iron ore. The reaction removes the sulfur, leaving purer iron with which to make steel. More magnesium is used in this way than in any other.

In some other processes, magnesium is combined with different metal ores so that it steals the oxygen from those ores, many of which are oxides. Among pure metals obtained this way are zinc, iron, titanium (Ti, element #22), and nickel (Ni, #28).

## The Rescuer

When water in the air or the ground combines with iron, the result is rust. This reddish-colored powder forms on iron and

Magnesium anodes have copper wire welded to the inside. Then the anodes are filled with tar to hold the connections in place. When the anodes are buried in the ground, the copper wire is attached to a steel structure to be protected. Electrons that would produce rust are, instead, sent through the wire to the anodes.

gradually weakens and destroys objects made of that metal. Magnesium can be used to extend the lives of large, expensive iron structures such as oil tanks, gas pipelines, or ship hulls.

Devices called magnesium anodes are connected to an iron structure. Electrons that would be used in forming rust are instead conducted to the anodes. Gradually, the magnesium turns into magnesium oxide and must be replaced. Because the magnesium wears away over time, this kind of protection is sometimes called sacrificial—the magnesium is being sacrificed to the steel tank or ship hull. It is easier and cheaper to replace the magnesium anodes than to replace the big steel structures.

## Lighting the Scene

The earliest photography could only be done outdoors on sunny days, because artificial light was not bright enough. It took the invention of a flash lamp to bring photography into the studio. The first flash lamp was invented in Germany in 1887. It used an open metal box or tray containing a powdered mixture of magnesium, potassium chlorate, and antimony sulfide (antimony is Sb, for *stibium*, element #51). When a flame touched the powder, it immediately flared into a bright, white light. The photographer had to take the picture quickly because the burning metals gave off not only light but also a cloud of smoke that could harm the photograph. The cloud wasn't smoke, though. It was finely powdered magnesium oxide, the result of the rapid oxidation of the metal.

In the 1920s, the small flashbulb was developed. Similar to an elec-

Fine filaments of magnesium metal are visible in this flash-bulb. When ignited by a small charge of electricity, they burn with a burst of brilliant light.

tric bulb, it was a glass envelope with fine magnesium wire inside it. The bulb was filled with oxygen. When the bulb was ignited by electricity, the metal burned very quickly, for as long as oxygen was available. The electrical mechanism controlling the flashbulb was connected to the camera, so that snapping the picture also ignited the flashbulb. Today, flashbulbs have generally been replaced by electronic flash attachments that do not use magnesium.

Some batteries are made with magnesium because they last a long time in storage. For example, flashlights that must be stored underground for emergency often use batteries that have magnesium and another element in the electrodes. A battery for use underwater uses the chemicals in the sea as the electrolyte.

Printing plates are made in a process called photoengraving. As it passes through film, light strikes light-sensitive chemicals on a metal plate. The chemicals etch, or eat away, the plate in patterns of light and dark that will eventually print as words and pictures. Magnesium has long been used as one of the metals for photoengraving.

## The Metal Goes Round and Round

In the 1950s and 1960s, the German automobile manufacturer Volkswagen used magnesium metal in its little cars, the Beetles. Each car contained about 21 kilograms (46 pounds) of magnesium. But when Volkswagen stopped manufacturing Beetles, the market for the metal dropped to almost nothing.

The primary use of magnesium became alloying with alu-

The first significant use of magnesium metal in a car was in this vehicle built for race driver Tommy Milton to drive in the Indianapolis 500. He won that 1921 race with an engine that used magnesium-alloy pistons.

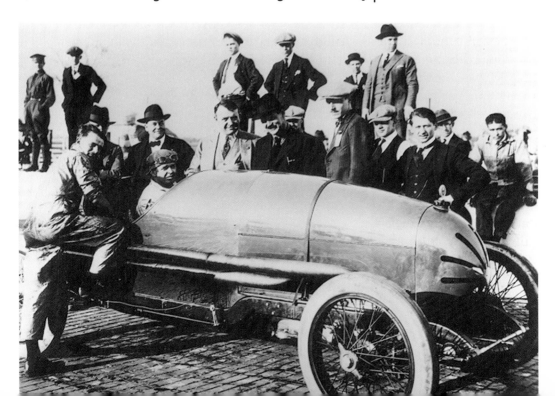

New race cars have magnesium structural parts that reduce weight and increase speed.

minum to make beverage cans. The side of an aluminum can contains only about 1.5 percent magnesium, and the can top, which has to be able to bend more, contains about 4.5 percent.

American carmakers were slow to use magnesium. The major reason it has not been used much is just that—it has not been used much. Companies do not know how to work the metal or even how to store it safely. The metal's major weakness has been that it does not hold up in places where great strength is needed or where the metal gets very hot when the engine is running. It starts to twist and change shape at only 150°C (302°F). New alloys are being developed to address these problems.

Most of the research into using magnesium has taken place in Europe, where the much higher cost of of gasoline has made the development of smaller, lighter cars more important than in the United States. It was not until the American people became more aware of the need to conserve petroleum and to reduce air pollution that magnesium gained in importance in the manufacture of automobiles.

Over the last 25 years, the amount of magnesium in the typical car has risen from 0.45 to 4.1 kilograms (1 pound to about 9 pounds), but it could easily go even higher. Magnesium could be especially useful in radiators and other parts where lighter weight would benefit fuel economy. At least one major American car manufacturer projects that by 2010, the average car will contain 23 to 46 kilograms (50 to 100 pounds) of magnesium. We will definitely be riding on element #12.

# A MAGNESIUM CATALOG

## Helping the Undersea World

Pollution and other consequences of human activity are destroying coral reefs all around the world. Some ocean scientists have created artificial coral reefs to which wandering corals and other marine invertebrates might attach themselves and begin the development of new reefs.

The most successful attempts have used a steel base on which humans have deposited calcium limestone and magnesium dolomite. These minerals are applied to the underlying metal by electrolysis. In years of observation, the living creatures that make real coral reefs have seemed to be just as satisfied by the human-made models. The electrolysis process has even been used to repair damaged reefs.

Scientists are studying coral reefs and how to save them. Dolomite deposited by electrolysis on human-made structures may help.

## The House Cat Problem

The digestive systems of house cats tend to accumulate crystals in the urinary tract. Called struvite, these crystals can cause a cat severe discomfort and even death. This condition is often blamed on too much magnesium in a cat's diet. Although some pet owners cut back on the amount of magnesium their cat receives, the crystals, which are calcium-based, can still form.

Crystal formation seems to have more to do with the acidity of the cat's urine than it does with magnesium. Urine needs to be slightly acidic, and, with a high-protein diet, it usually is. If the urine becomes alkaline, or basic, certain ions in the urine can start to crystallize and turn into struvite. This can happen when a cat eats commercial food that contains more vegetable matter than protein and receives insufficient water. Dry cat food (which many people give their cats because it's good for their teeth) can be moistened with water to increase the cat's water intake.

## The Queen's Ruby

Spinel is a gemstone consisting of magnesium aluminum oxide, $MgAl_2O_4$. The variety called ruby spinel is a beautiful deep red and is sometimes mistaken for real ruby. Spinels are not as hard or heavy as real ruby, which is aluminum oxide, without the magnesium. Spinels are found mostly in Southeast Asia, in Myanmar (formerly Burma), Sri Lanka, and Thailand. They can also be created in a laboratory.

The world's largest red gemstone is called the Timur ruby, though it is a spinel. It is set in the

**Although this spinel is not red, its cubic shape makes it rare.**

imperial crown of the United Kingdom, which Queen Elizabeth wears for state occasions.

## Second is Good

The drills that geologists use to locate petroleum and other minerals have to be a lot harder than the rock they cut through. For this reason, scientists at the U.S. Department of Energy have been working to develop a very hard material to be used in cutting tools. They have developed a compound that is a combination of aluminum, magnesium, and boron, made even harder by a little bit of silicon. They say that this material is now the second-hardest substance known. Diamond remains the hardest.

## Magnesium Bicycles

One-piece welded bicycle frames of 94 percent magnesium have been produced since the late 1990s in Europe and Taiwan (the other 6 percent of the frame material is a business secret). The material has the highest weight-to-strength ratio of all common metals. It quickly replaced carbon fiber as the most desirable bicycle frame material. The problem that kept magnesium from being used in this way sooner was the fact that the metal corrodes so easily, reacting both to air and water.

**The magnesium frame for this bicycle is cast in a single piece of metal and weighs only about 2.7 kilograms (6 pounds).**

Magnesium bicycles have an added benefit in that the material does not vibrate in response to rough surfaces as readily as other materials. Vibration contributes to a rider's fatigue.

## Clearing the Roads

Common salt—sodium chloride, NaCl—has long been used on icy roads to melt ice so that wheels don't spin. Unfortunately, when this salt melts and runs off the road, it can damage trees and other plants alongside the road. The chemicals can also get into waterways, where the additional sodium can harm water supplies.

In the 1980s, chemists working for the Federal Highway Administration developed a new chemical—calcium magnesium acetate, or CMA. It does the same job as salt but does not harm living things. In fact, it's been suggested that the substance is even good for trees because both calcium and magnesium are needed by plants. The substance also does less damage to metal bridges and cars, which are corroded by salt. That fact alone may encourage municipalities to use it—not an easy decision because CMA costs much more than salt.

The chemists who first worked with CMA used equal amounts of calcium and magnesium. However, they found the chemical worked even better when they used more magnesium than calcium because magnesium has a lower freezing point, which made the chemical more useful.

## Future Fuel on the Road

The combustion, or burning, of gasoline in an automobile engine creates many substances that are harmful to the environment. The combustion of hydrogen creates only water, so hydrogen engines are an idea whose time will most likely come. The problem is how to package the hydrogen so that it is practical. One answer might be hydrides.

This environmentally aware driver is fueling his car with liquid hydrogen. The car's trunk contains a special, very strong tank where the gas is stored before use in the engine.

Hydrides are chemicals that combine one or more metallic elements with hydrogen. Magnesium readily binds with hydrogen in compounds such as magnesium hydride, $MgH_2$ and $MgNiH_4$. Automotive engineers are interested in hydrides as a possible fuel of the future. Many people think hydrogen will eventually replace gasoline in powering car engines. But hydrogen in its gaseous form takes up a lot of room. When compressed to take up less room, hydrogen needs a storage tank that is very strong.

A substance that contains hydrogen to be released when the engine runs is more efficient. Hydrides might be the answer. At the high temperature created in a car engine, the hydrogen separates from the metal. The hydrogen can then be piped into the engine for combustion. Magnesium hydrides are ideal because of their lightness. However, they require higher heat than an engine normally makes to break apart. A solution to this problem is being sought.

## Future Fuel in Space

Magnesium has long been used in pyrotechnic rockets, or fireworks. But now rocket scientists are looking at the possibility of using magnesium, not in the casing of a rocket but as part of the propellant, or fuel. In early rocketry, powdered aluminum was used in solid fuel because it was less expensive than magnesium and nearly as reactive (it has three valence electrons instead of two).

It would not be practical to use magnesium in the propellant of a rocket designed to leave Earth because it would burn too fast. But the fuel might work in a small rocket to be launched from a colony of humans working on the moon or another planet. A nongovernment firm, Wickman Spacecraft & Propulsion Company, has developed a small rocket engine that uses materials found on other planets as fuel. Mars, for example, is known to have magnesium in its surface soil. Wickman's rocket might burn fuel of powdered magnesium mixed with carbon dioxide.

**A rocket engine that burns fuel made of magnesium and carbon dioxide is being test-fired.**

# Magnesium in Brief

**Name:** Magnesium, after the mineral magnesite, which was named for Magnesia, a region in ancient Greece

**Symbol:** Mg

**Discoverer:** Sir Humphry Davy in 1808

**Atomic number:** 12

**Atomic weight:** 24.305

**Electrons in the shells:** 2, 8, 2

**Group:** 2 (also called IIA), the alkaline-earth metals; other elements in Group 2, with 2 electrons in the outer shell, include beryllium, calcium, strontium, barium, and radium

**Usual characteristics:** soft, malleable, silvery-white metal that oxidizes rapidly

**Density (mass per unit volume):** 1.738 grams per cubic centimeter

**Melting point (freezing point):** 650°C (1,202°F)

**Boiling point (liquefaction point):** 1,090 °C.(1,994°F)

**Abundance:**

    **Universe:** eighth most abundant element

    **Earth's crust:** about 2.5% by weight; fifth most abundant element

    **Seawater:** 0.13%; third most abundant ion

    **Human body:** 0.50%; fourth most abundant element, half of it in bone

**Naturally occurring stable isotopes:** Mg-24 (78.9%), Mg-25 (10%), and Mg-26 (11.1%)

**Artificial radioactive isotopes:** Mg-20 to -23 and Mg-27 to -31

# Glossary

**acid:** definitions vary, but basically it is a corrosive substance that gives up a positive hydrogen ion (H+), equal to a proton when dissolved in water; indicates less than 7 on the pH scale because of its large number of hydrogen ions

**alkali:** a substance, such as an hydroxide or carbonate of an alkali metal, that when dissolved in water causes an increase in the hydroxide ion (OH-) concentration, forming a basic solution.

**anion:** an ion with a negative charge

**anode:** a negative electrode

**atom:** the smallest amount of an element that exhibits the properties of the element, consisting of protons, electrons, and (usually) neutrons

**base:** a substance that accepts a hydrogen ion (H+) when dissolved in water; indicates higher than 7 on the pH scale because of its small number of hydrogen ions

**boiling point:** the temperature at which a liquid at normal pressure evaporates into a gas, or a solid changes directly (sublimes) into a gas

**bond:** the attractive force linking atoms together in a molecule or crystal

**catalyst:** a substance that causes or speeds a chemical reaction without itself being consumed in the reaction

**cathode:** a positive electrode

**cation:** an ion with a positive charge

**chemical reaction:** a transformation or change in a substance involving the electrons of the chemical elements making up the substance

**compound:** a substance formed by two or more chemical elements bound together by chemical means

**crystal:** a solid substance in which the atoms are arranged in three-dimensional patterns that create smooth outer surfaces, or faces

**decompose:** to break down a substance into its components

**density:** the amount of material in a given volume, or space; mass per unit volume; often stated as grams per cubic centimeter (g/cm³)

**dissolve:** to spread evenly throughout the volume of another substance

**distillation:** the process in which a liquid is heated until it evaporates and the gas is collected and condensed back into a liquid in another container; often used to separate mixtures into their different components

**DNA:** deoxyribonucleic acid, a chemical in the nucleus of each living cell, which carries genetic information

**electrode:** a device such as a metal plate that conducts electrons into or out of a solution or battery

**electrolysis:** the decomposition of a substance by electricity

**electrolyte:** a substance that when dissolved in water or when liquefied conducts electricity

**element:** a substance that cannot be split chemically into simpler substances that maintain the same characteristics. Each of the 103 naturally occurring chemical elements is made up of atoms of the same kind.

**enzyme:** one of the many complex proteins that act as biological catalysts in the body

**evaporate:** to change from a liquid to a gas

**gas:** a state of matter in which the atoms or molecules move freely, matching the shape and volume of the container holding it

**group:** a vertical column in the Periodic Table, with each element having similar physical and chemical characteristics; also called chemical family

**half-life:** the period of time required for half of a radioactive element to decay

**hormone:** any of various secretions of the endocrine glands that control different functions of the body, especially at the cellular level

**ion:** an atom or molecule that has acquired an electric charge by gaining or losing one or more electrons

**ionic bond:** a link between two atoms made by one atom taking one or more electrons from the other, giving the two atoms opposite electrical charges, which holds them together

**isotope:** an atom with a different number of neutrons in its nucleus from other atoms of the same element

**mass number:** the total of protons and neutrons in the nucleus of an atom

**melting point:** the temperature at which a solid becomes a liquid

**metal:** a chemical element that conducts electricity, usually shines, or reflects light, is dense, and can be shaped. About three-quarters of the naturally occurring elements are metals.

**metalloid:** a chemical element that has some characteristics of a metal and some of a nonmetal; includes some elements in Groups 13 through 17 in the Periodic Table

**molecule:** the smallest amount of a substance that has the characteristics of the substance and usually consists of two or more atoms

**monomer:** a molecule that can be linked to many other identical molecules to make a polymer

**neutral:** 1) having neither acidic nor basic properties; 2) having no electrical charge

**neutron:** a subatomic particle within the nucleus of all atoms except hydrogen; has no electric charge

**nonmetal:** a chemical element that does not conduct electricity, is not dense, and is too brittle to be worked. Nonmetals easily form ions, and they include some elements in Groups 14 through 17 and all of Group 18 in the Periodic Table.

**nucleus:** 1) the central part of an atom, which has a positive electrical charge from its one or more protons; the nuclei of all atoms except hydrogen also include electrically neutral neutrons; 2) the central portion of most living cells, which controls the activities of the cells and contains the genetic material

**oxidation:** the loss of electrons during a chemical reaction; need not necessarily involve the element oxygen

**pH:** a measure of the acidity of a substance, on a scale of 0 to 14, with 7 being neutral. The abbreviation pH stands for "potential of hydrogen."

**photosynthesis:** in green plants, the process by which carbon dioxide and water, in the presence of light, are turned into sugars

**pressure:** the force exerted by an object divided by the area over which the force is exerted. The air at sea level exerts a pressure, called atmospheric pressure, of 14.7 pounds per square inch (1013 millibars).

**protein:** a complex biological chemical made by the linking of many amino acids

**proton:** a subatomic particle within the nucleus of all atoms; has a positive electric charge

**radioactive:** of an atom, spontaneously emitting high-energy particles

**reduction:** the gain of electrons, which occurs in conjunction with oxidation

**respiration:** the process of taking in oxygen and giving off carbon dioxide

**salt:** any compound that, with water, results from the neutralization of an acid by a base. In common usage, sodium chloride (table salt)

**shell:** a region surrounding the nucleus of an atom in which one or more electrons can occur. The inner shell can hold a maximum of two electrons; others may hold eight or more. If an atom's outer, or valence, shell does not hold its maximum number of electrons, the atom is subject to chemical reactions.

**solid:** a state of matter in which the shape of the collection of atoms or molecules does not depend on the container

**solution:** a mixture in which one substance is evenly distributed throughout another

**sublime:** to change directly from a solid to a gas without becoming a liquid first

**ultraviolet:** electromagnetic radiation which has a wavelength shorter than visible light

**valence electron:** an electron located in the outer shell of an atom, available to participate in chemical reactions

**vitamin:** any of several organic substances, usually obtainable from a balanced diet, that the human body needs for specific physiological processes to take place

# For Further Information

## BOOKS

Atkins, P. W. *The Periodic Kingdom: A Journey into the Land of the Chemical Elements.* NY: Basic Books, 1995

Heiserman, David L. *Exploring Chemical Elements and Their Compounds,* Blue Ridge Summit, PA: Tab Books, 1992

Hoffman, Roald, and Vivian Torrence. *Chemistry Imagined: Reflections on Science.* Washington, DC: Smithsonian Institution Press, 1993

Newton, David E. *Chemical Elements.* Venture Books. Danbury, CT: Franklin Watts, 1994

Yount, Lisa. *Antoine Lavoisier: Founder of Modern Chemistry.* "Great Minds of Science" series. Springfield, NJ: Enslow Publishers, 1997

## CD-ROM

*Discover the Elements: The Interactive Periodic Table of the Chemical Elements,* Paradigm Interactive, Greensboro, NC, 1995

## INTERNET SITES

Note that useful sites on the Internet can change and even disappear. If the following site addresses do not work, use a search engine that you find useful, such as:
Yahoo:

http://www.yahoo.com

or AltaVista:

http://altavista.digital.com

A very thorough listing of the major characteristics, uses, and compounds of all the chemical elements can be found at a site called WebElements:

http://www.shef.ac.uk/~chem/we b-elements/

A Canadian site on the Nature of the Environment includes a large section on the elements in the various Earth systems:

http://www.cent.org/geo12/geo12/htm

Colored photos of various molecules, cells, and biological systems can be viewed at:

http://www.clarityconnect.com/webpages/-cramer/PictureIt/welcome.htm

Many subjects are covered on WWW Virtual Library. It also includes a useful collection of links to other sites:

http://www.earthsystems.org/Environment/shtml

# INDEX

neutrons 11, 13
Nevada 16
Nicholson, William 9
nickel 47
nitrogen 26, 27
Nobel Prize 25-26
nucleus 10-11, 13
nutrients 29, 35
nuts 44

ocean 14, 20-22, 52
olivine 19-20
open-hearth process 47
orange tree 29
orbits 11-12
organic catalysts 36
orthoclase 17
osteoporosis 35
oxidation 49, 58
oxides 47
oxygen 9, 12-13, 19-
  20, 25, 29, 40, 47-49

pancreas 38-39
paralysis 31
parathyroid gland 37
parathyroid hormone
  37
Pelletier, Pierre 25
periclase 15
peridot 19
Periodic Table of the
  Elements 11, 13, 58
petroleum 47, 51, 54
pharmacist 25
phosphates 35, 42
phosphorus 35-36
photoengraving 50
photography 12, 48-49
photosynthesis 25-26,
  28, 30, 38
Piccard, Jean and
  Auguste 47
pigments 27-28
pistons 46
plants 20, 24-25, 27,
  29, 30-31, 36, 38, 55

plasma 37-38
poison 25, 42
pollution 51-52
porphyrin ring 26-28
potassium 9, 14, 30-31,
  33, 35, 42, 44
potassium chlorate 49
precipitation 22
printing plates 50
propellant 57
protein 37, 53
protons 10-11, 13
pyrotechnics 46, 57

quartz 17
Queen Elizabeth 54

race car 50, 51
radiation 28
radiators 51
radioactive isotopes
  13, 58
radioactive material 26
radium 11, 58
rain 20, 48
reactive metal 12
red blood cells 25
refractories 46-47
resins 23
retina 12
ribonucleic acid (RNA)
  32, 33
rocketry 57
ruby spinel 53-54
rust 47-48

salt 20-23, 55
salt pellets 23
sand 13
scale 23
scarabs 17
scientists 11, 20, 25,
  31, 32, 52, 54, 57
Scotland 9
sea 13, 15
seashells 15
sedimentary rock 15

serpentine asbestos 18
ships 48
silicates 19
silicon 13, 16, 18-19,
  54
silicon dioxide 13
skin 8, 34
slag 16
small intestine 39
soapstone 16-17
sodium 9, 20-21, 23,
  35, 45, 55
sodium chloride 20, 55
soft water 23, 30
soil 20, 29-30, 57
solar system 15, 46
Southeast Asia 53
Soviet Union 14
spa 8, 11
spacecraft 45
spinal cord 42
spinal tap 41
spinel 53-54
Sri Lanka 53
starches 29
steel 47-48, 52
stibium 49
stomach 31, 33
stress 38, 42
stroke 40-41, 43
strontium 9, 11, 58
struvite 53
strychnine 25
sugar 25, 29, 36, 38-
  39, 44
sulfates 19
sulfur 11, 47
sunlight 24-25, 28, 34
suspension 33
Switzerland 25
synthesis 33

tailings 18
Taiwan 54
talc 16-17
talcum powder 16-17
tall fescue 31

teeth 33, 35
Texas 22
Thailand 53
thermal reduction 16
thorium 46
Timur ruby 53-54
titanium 47
toothpaste 17

United Kingdom 54
United States 16, 18,
  25, 39, 46, 51, 54
University of California
  at Berkeley 26
urinary tract 53
urine 34, 42, 53

valence shell 11-12, 57
vapor 10
vegetables 44, 53
Venera spacecraft 14-
  15
Venus 14-15
vertebrae 42
vitamin D 34
Volkswagen 50
Volta, Alessandro 9
voltaic cell 9
Von Sachs, Julius 25

waste chemicals 47
water 8-9, 13, 15, 19-
  24, 28, 30, 33, 41, 42,
  47, 48, 53, 55
water softeners 23, 30
water vapor 19
water-treatment 47
wheat 43
Wickman Spacecraft &
  Propulsion Co. 57
Willstätter, Richard 25
Woodward, Robert
  Burns 26
World War I 46
World War II 13

zinc 46-47